ARCHIBALD KNOX
AND
MARY SETON WATTS

'MODERN CELTIC ART'
GARDEN POTTERY

Veronica Franklin Gould

BOOK OF GARDEN ORNAMENTS

BY

LIBERTY & Cᴼ LONDON & PARIS

CONTENTS

PIONEERS OF 'MODERN CELTIC ART' GARDEN POTTERY

'Never before, in this country at least, has the Garden Pot been treated as an item, *per se*, of decorative skill,' declared Liberty & Co. in its first *Book of Garden Ornaments*. That the company name was internationally recognised for its decorative arts style was due in part to its policy of keeping designers anonymous. However, Arthur Lasenby Liberty, outraged that the spread of Continental Art Nouveau was vulgarising Liberty style, broke the policy. He named the craftswoman Mary Seton Watts (1849-1938) – or as his catalogues described her, 'Mrs G. F. Watts, talented wife of our greatest living artist' – as the prime mover of his latest range.[1] Exotic terracotta garden pottery, designed by both Archibald Knox (1864-1933) and Mary Watts, offered for sale in Liberty & Co.'s *Yule-Tide Gifts* catalogue of 1903-4, was shown in March 1904 in the company's landmark exhibition, *Modern Celtic Art* at the Grafton Galleries in Bond Street, London; and among the displays were Cymric silver, Tudric pewter, jewellery and carpets, many of which were designed by the prolific, unnamed Knox.[2]

The two designers, both outwardly reserved, burned with imaginative impulses aroused by remote Celtic homelands – hers was a Highland castle overlooking Loch Ness, and Knox was born and brought up on the Isle of Man – which they viewed with painterly passion. For their modern designs, they drew inspiration from lights and shadows thrown by nature and Celtic knot patterns, the intertwining curves and

Archibald Knox, c. 1910
(Manx National Heritage).

G. F. Watts, *Mary Seton
Watts*, 1886 (Watts Gallery).

symbols worked by ancient craftsmen. Looking further back than the medievalist theorists of the Arts and Crafts movement, Augustus Welby Northmore Pugin (1812-52), John Ruskin (1819-1900) and William Morris (1834-96), they broke new ground in their fulfilment of Arts and Crafts ideals.

Watts, a fervent socialist despite her privileged background, wholeheartedly embraced the principle of uniting artist and craftsman. A national campaigner for the widespread amateur craft revival movement, the Home Arts and Industries Association, she had set up professional pottery workshops at her home in Compton, Surrey, with a branch in Inverness-shire.[3] Whether Liberty & Co. credited her because of her famous husband, the Academician George Frederic Watts, or because her ornaments, made by and for her own pottery, were not commissioned for the company, this rare acknowledgement has led to a misconception that Knox terracotta was produced at Compton. Once Knox had submitted his designs to Liberty & Co., as far as we know, he played no part in the execution of the pots; but it is fitting that the two designers were exhibited together, with respect to their contrasting interpretation of Celtic art.

The son of Scottish parents living on the Isle of Man, Knox was educated at Douglas Grammar School, where he became a pupil teacher of art. In 1883, the new headmaster Canon John Quine, a scholarly archaeologist, opened his eyes to the cultural heritage of the island[4] – the natural and artistic roots of Knox's design work. At the Douglas School of Art, he learned from the artist John Miller Nicholson to view the model 'from all sides, above, below, touching it, gathering through our fingertips what we might not discern with our eyes;[5] and the headmaster W. J. Merrit passed on avant-garde ideas taught by the naturalistic French sculptor Aimée-Jules Dalou, a leading figure in the New Sculpture movement.[6] Dalou gave dynamic clay-modelling demonstrations at the Slade and the South Kensington Art-Training School in London, showing students – among them Mary Fraser Tytler (the future Mrs Watts) – how sculpture should come from within the heart of the clay rather than the surface.[7]

By 1884, Knox was appointed art master at Douglas, where he won medals for his specialist subject, Celtic ornament. Through the local archaeological society, he met Philip Kermode and is said to have supplied illustrations for his authoritative study on Manx crosses, published in 1887.[8] In 1893 – presumably, at the instigation of the architect Mackay Hugh Baillie Scott, for whom he was now working part-time – Knox had his own study of the tenth-century crosses carved by Gaut, the son of Biarn of Cooley, printed in the *Builder*.[9] It was to these early Viking carvings of ring-chain knotwork, known as the Borre style after a Norwegian gold hoard, that Knox referred in his designs for terracotta. Baillie Scott, who wrote for the *Studio*, the new arts journal to which Knox himself would contribute in 1896,[10] gave him first-hand training in the conception and fulfilment of Arts and Crafts architecture, and the integral harmony of its decoration and where deviations might be valid. For example, the architect's Douglas home, noted for its harmonious flowing space, robust oak beams and carved newel posts, was built of red bricks and clay tiles that were not indigenous to the island. According to Hermann Muthesius in *Das Englische Haus* (1904), Baillie Scott was the first architect 'to have realised the interior as an autonomous work of art'.[11]

Knox travelled to Dublin to delve deeper into the art of the Celts and collected photographs of bronze and gold objects – now in the National Museum – whose shapes he looked to for his terracotta jardinières. In Christopher Dresser's studio in Barnes, Knox learned the latest design techniques and an introduction to the nearby Silver Studio in Hammersmith; and 1897 found him in Surrey, teaching at the Redhill School of Art and supplying the Silver Studio with designs for textiles and wallpapers, the first of which was bought by Liberty & Co. in 1898. His Celtic roots were never far from his heart and he published an article on 'Old Kirk Lonan' in the *Antiquary*.[12]

Borre knotwork, Isle of Man, (*Builder*, 1893):

Left: Malumkun's Cross, Kirk Michael.

Far left: St Katherine's Cross, Oncham.

Left:
Watts Chapel
Compton,
1895-98.

Opposite:
Watts Chapel
doorway
(detail).

On 4 July, Knox's local newspaper, the *Surrey Advertiser*, reported the consecration of a mortuary chapel in Compton, twenty miles west of Redhill. An exuberant terracotta structure imbued with Celtic symbolism, the form and decoration and decoration of the Watts Chapel extends the motif favoured by Gaut, but which its architect traced back to Ephesus and Sanskrit – a circle, universal symbol of eternity intersected by a cross that represents love stretching to the corners of the earth.[13] Transepts pierce and rise above the drum. Designed by Mary Seton Watts and modelled under her tuition by villagers, it was the subject of an illustrated article in the *Studio*, which had regularly featured its symbolic tiles in reports on the Home Arts exhibitions at the Royal Albert Hall.[14] So extensive were her influences and so exuberant her designs that they did not produce the impression of repose that Knox himself sought in his own work. Nor was that the intention, for into her Celtic knots, enlivened by higher-relief Art Nouveau figures, Watts incorporated pantheistic symbolism – motifs from Buddhism, Hinduism, Judaism, Assyria, Egypt, Persia –

8

in order that the chapel should provide sanctuary to people of all creeds. Ruskin's *Queen of the Air* had been her point of departure and the ninth-century *Book of Kells*, and British Museum bronzes, her chief Celtic sources. Her symbols, intended to suggest ideas, conveyed multiple meanings. Curiosity would surely have drawn Knox to inspect the chapel, though its architect had spirited herself away to her family home in Scotland.

Mary Seton Fraser Tytler was born on 25 November 1849 at Ahmednaggar in India. Her father Charles, a civil servant with the East India Company, spent his spare time writing treatises on prophecy and the Apocalypse. Mary, the third daughter of a sporting Episcopalian family, was brought up by her grandparents and educated by governesses at Aldourie, near Dores, in Inverness-shire, where her grandfather William Fraser Tytler held court as Sheriff. Ghostly battles were often seen nearby and a witch was known to trouble the locals. As Mary grew up, the house was transformed into a baronial-style castle. Its walls were decorated with hunting trophies and family portraits painted by the finest Scottish artists; there were relics from the battle of Culloden and the library shelves were filled with historic manuscripts: her great-great-grandfather's defence of Mary Queen of Scots, her great-uncle Patrick Fraser Tytler's nine-volume *History of Scotland* (1828-43) and poems handwritten by Robert Burns and Sir Walter Scott. As aware of her ancestral links with the poetic soul of Scotland as its often violent history, she inherited her esoteric vision from Alexander Fraser Tytler, Lord Woodhouselee, the Judge of Session and former professor of universal history at Edinburgh University, who in 1790 published a study of 'Extraordinary Structures on the Tops of Hills in the Highlands with Remarks on the Progress of the Arts among the Ancient Inhabitants.'[15] A century later, his great granddaughter would create an exotic

Church leaders of England,
Scotland, Ireland and Wales,
c. 1867, in Mary
Fraser Tytler's album
(Watts Gallery).

architecture and garden ornaments inspired by the art of ancient civilizations, which she bound together with the Celtic cord of unity.[16]

When Mary was twelve, her father returned from India and moved his family to Sanquhar, near Forres in Morayshire. The Celtic King Duff was murdered in A.D. 965; and a stone marks the spot where the three witches accused of causing his death were burned. However, it was the symbolism of Sueno's Stone, a Pictish obelisk carved with foliate interlace and battle scenes of massed armies and slaughter[17] – the battle of life and the triumph of good over evil – that she was to infuse into her adult decorative work.

As a teenager, Mary embraced the Victorian vogue for decorating her photograph album with imaginative watercolour settings for *cartes de visite*.[18] Her skilful use of ornament indicates that she was receiving professional tuition, presumably at the new Inverness art school. In 1868, during a family holiday in Freshwater on the Isle of Wight, she sat to the photographer Julia Margaret Cameron and was at once set to work, modelling props. Two years later, on her return from art studies in Dresden and Rome, Mary visited the studio of George Frederic Watts, the controversial Symbolist and distinguished portrait painter, whom she regarded as the finest modern artist. She enrolled at the South Kensington Art-Training School and in 1872 entered the Slade. Over the years she took her work to Mr. Watts and became his unofficial student, painting portraits and learning from pictures at his Little Holland House Gallery in Kensington. On 20 November 1886, three days before her 37th birthday, she married the 69-year-old artist.[19]

Obliged to give up the clay-modelling evening classes she had started for shoeblacks in Whitechapel under a scheme run by the Reverend Samuel Barnett and affiliated to the Home Arts, she joined her husband as a council member. The idea of the Home Arts was to train volunteers to teach woodcarving, mosaic, lace-making, metalwork, bookbinding or weaving, to the working classes, to rescue them from idleness, gambling and drinking, to open their eyes to beauty and the joy of creativity and give them a new chance in life. Their work was exhibited annually at the Royal Albert Hall and the ideal – rarely achieved – was to turn them into professional craftsmen.[20]

Watts, intimidated by her husband's fame, gave up painting and resolved instead to design decorative art to symbolise the universal thoughts – of Love, Life and Death – that his life and work inspired. At Limnerslease in Compton, Surrey, she modelled ceiling decorations of gesso patterns based on symbols from ancient civilisations. Researching at the British Museum, Watts became enchanted by spirals on

Celtic bronzes and the story-telling style of the *Book of Kells*. She wove her pantheistic symbols into a Celtic cord of unity, developing an intricate, yet harmonious style.

At her aunt's graveside in October 1893, the ugly stone sparked the idea that she might teach people to create their own memorials from terracotta and brick, or stone, depending on resources and architecture of the area. Watts planned to ask artist friends for designs. As the wife of an influential Academician and key promoter of the craft revival, she had direct access to the finest artist-craftsmen in the country. Among their visitors that day were C. R. Ashbee, founder of the Guild and School of Handicrafts and Walter Crane, president of the Arts and Crafts Exhibition Society.[21] Burne-Jones had organised Osmund Weeks, who prepared Crane's gesso, to assist her; and while Crane was sitting for his portrait, she took her design work into her husband's studio to take full advantage. When the opportunity arose to engage villagers in the creation an entire memorial chapel for Compton's new cemetery, she located a seam of gault clay nearby, designed models in cardboard and clay, sought advice

Watts, *Wisdom*, 1891, gesso, Limnerslease, Compton.

on her kiln from William De Morgan, commandeered assistants from her husband's sculpture studio and in November 1895 her Terra Cotta Home Arts classes began.[22]

By March 1898, the highly symbolic chapel was built and its exterior decoration complete. Watts realised that her potters had achieved the Home Arts ideal, for as her cynosure Ruskin had written in *The Seven Lamps of Architecture*, 'a piece of terracotta wrought by human hand … is worth all the stone in Carrara cut by machinery.'[23] The chapel's coarsely-modelled friezes, broken by shadow to achieve the sublime expression of sympathy and sorrow, and integral to the form and overall concept of the building, embodied Arts and Crafts philosophy so successfully that Watts began to plan a professional enterprise. For profitable use of the kiln, she decided to produce three ranges: tombstones, sundials and garden pots and she would draw on the iconographic vocabulary established in the chapel. She supervised the modelling of her designs, directing the shape until a satisfactory prototype was achieved and moulds made for production.[24]

Her first tombstone, modelled on 28 March by Thomas Steadman, was inspired by a pattern in the Library of Saint Gall, embellished with a ring of cherubs, their intertwining wings surrounding a Celtic wheel cross and knot roundel. Two days later, Louis Deuchars modelled the capital for her *Winged Hours* sundial. Cherubs face north, south, east and west, suggesting the idea of the cross, but here Watts requested they smile and frown 'It gives it a touch of the human.' Steadman modelled the *Peacock* sundial, intended to represent 'the three steps of the sun'; for the morning, a cock, Early Christian symbol for watchfulness, for noon, a peacock, Buddhist and Brahmin symbol of immortality, and for evening, an owl symbolising truth and wisdom. Liberty & Co. renamed all her terracotta ware in the *Book of Garden Ornaments* where the above sundials appear as the *St Andrew* and the *Owl* and

Left: *Peacock* sundial,
1898*

Top: Capital of *Winged
Hours* sundial, 1898*

Above: Memorial,
Compton, 1895

* dates of Watts's original design

15

her elegant *Scroll* pot, often misattributed to Gertrude Jekyll, as *Wottan*. Its curly round handle appears to have developed from Watts's drawings of Egyptian scarab designs and her own favourite heart motif. Like Knox, she designed many knot variations on the Celtic cross of hearts. The curvilinear terracotta seats decorated with pierced abstract strapwork and placed outside the chapel are perhaps closest to his style. The altar, in itself a Celtic Revival masterpiece, was surrounded by sundials and pots at the Home Arts exhibition in May 1899.[25]

It was either at the Home Arts or in Scotland that summer, that Watts met James Morton. Alexander Morton & Co, suppliers of art textiles to Liberty & Co., had set up the workshop in co-operation with the Irish Congested Districts Board, in order to create employment. Morton commissioned Watts to design a hearth rug to be hand-tufted in Killibegs,

Terracotta seats outside the Watts Chapel, 1898.

16

Scroll pot,
1898, Potters'
Arts Guild mark.

County Donegal. In December 1899, she wrote to the weavers to explain that, carrying on the heritage of their ancestors, they were weaving motifs that related to cultures throughout the world. The *Pelican* rug, named after the bird that wounded its chest to feed its young, symbolised 'the love which will give its own heart's blood to help those who suffer or are in need'; and the 'T' symbol, carved by the first Christians on Irish and on Gaelic stone crosses, was also used by the Egyptians to signify the 'Key of Life', symbol of immortality. 'It is here on our rug to remind us in our earthly home of eternity.'[26]

By December 1900, Watts reported to Morton that the Aldourie branch of her pottery was in full swing. Under instruction from Deuchars, young Highlanders were producing her garden pots from Inverness-shire clay. Watts came to regard Morton as her 'knight of commerce'. He helped her find a Scottish manager for Compton and negotiated terms with James Nicol, who came down from the

Cumnock Pottery in Glasgow, in January 1901. Her Donegal carpet and Agriculture and Technical Instruction stand at the 1901 Glasgow International Exhibition. Morton, keen to pursue the Celtic style, sought Watts's advice. That March she sent him a wide-ranging book list headed by the *Book of Kells* and covering Scottish monuments, Early Christian symbolism, South Kensington Museum handbooks on the arts of Denmark and Scandinavia and Celtic art by Margaret Stokes who, Watts pointed out, was bringing out a series of articles on Ireland's high crosses.

'How glad I am that you are going to *carry forward* the Celtic art – it is our own and was left incomplete – I love it with all my heart and ... we in the present day should not be mere *copyists* of their elaborate knottings or half thought out, though beautiful and original

Watts, *Pelican* rug (detail), 1899-1900 (Watts Gallery).

18

designs, but breathe its spirit ... use it as a language in which our modern thoughts can be conveyed, *invent* upon it ...There is no decoration so suited to *telling* its story. It is, I believe, like the gaelic language, the most emotional of the styles of decoration. But has the dangers common to all highly emotional things and requires reserve and temperance and judgement, in the soul of the designer, to prevent it from becoming meaningless.'[27]

Knox and C. F. A. Voysey were subsequently commissioned to send Celtic-style designs for Donegal carpets which Liberty & Co. promoted in an exhibition *Founding a National Industry – Irish Carpets* at the Grafton Gallery in March 1903.[28]

Knox had returned to the Isle of Man in 1900 and was living in Sulby, designing Celtic-inspired memorial crosses, when he was commissioned by Liberty & Co. to design terracotta garden ornaments. Prototypes from his drawings were modelled in red Surrey clay, by James Radley Young at Hammer Vale Pottery in Haslemere. In the period leading up to the *Modern Celtic Art* exhibition, between 11 February 1903 and 3 March 1904, Liberty & Co. registered fourteen Knox designs and Watts registered hers on 14 May 1903. Catalogue announcements that 'the present exhibitors have struck out into untrodden paths ... largely aided and advised by Mrs G. F. Watts,' with 'Notes from the Workshop' that refer only to her Home Arts class at Limnerslease, Compton, has led to the assumption that the Knox terracotta was also produced at Compton, but Watts did not yet know his name. His pots were made from the coarser salmon, buff and darker red clay – the colour varying according to the iron oxide content – dug from Carter & Co.'s Corfe Mullen beds and produced at their East Quay works in Poole, Dorset. Radley Young carried

The faience department at Carter & Co, with a *Balder* jardinière,
designed by Archibald Knox, 1903-4, in the centre, beside the pedestal.

Liberty & Co., *Yule-Tide Gifts*, terracotta, 1903-4:
Watts: nos. 1 *Floreal* pot; 3, *Fafnir* pot; 8, unnamed window box;
11 *Gudrun* pot and stand; 12, *Pomono* pot and stand.
Knox: nos. 2 *Olaf* pot and pedestal; 4, *Sigurd* pot and pedestals;
6, *Beowulf* pot and pedestal; 7 *Brunhild* pot and *Gnomme* pedestal;
9, *Thrym* pot; 10, *Grimhild* pot and stand combined.

20

out commissions for Carter's, his former employers to whom he returned full-time in 1906. After moulds were made from his prototypes, terracotta jardinières, pedestals and balustrades were stamped with the Liberty mark and registration number and went into a coal-fired kiln. [29]

Under Nicol's supervision at Compton, clay was dug, weathered and treated to withstand frost and the kiln was fired by wood to give the terracotta 'a delicate and broken colour.'[30] Pots were impressed on the outside with a symbolic two-inch wheel mark intended to embody the potters' work and aspirations – 'THEIR WORK AS IT WERE A WHEEL IN THE MIDDLE OF A WHEEL' with 'LIMNERSLEASE / COMPTON' or 'ALDOURIE / DORES.' Within the wheel of labour, wings suggest the value of handwork and thought 'the spiritual flight into the unseen,' an inner wheel and Celtic knot suggest shelter, protection, movement and life and show that the wheel of life should move 'sunwise.'[31] Watts, a dedicated Christian, abhorred narrow doctrine and, rather like her approach to the use of symbols, picked up broader aspects from Buddhist, Hindu or Jewish teachings.[32]

Compton Potters'
Arts Guild wheel mark.

21

Knox, a devout Anglo-Catholic, stressed the importance of imaginative thought in the creation of his designs. Watts would have thoroughly endorsed his description of design as 'the imagination choosing, endeavouring to bring, by aid of art, things of nature into harmony with the things of the mind … form containing always material for new and other form; suggestive, incomplete, the imagination never rests.'[33] At Kingston School of Art where Knox was head of design in 1899, returning there from the Isle of Man in 1904, he taught that there were two natures: 'Outside Nature and Our Own, the last being Art. Art the outcome and reward of practice and study.'[34] But unlike Watts whose exuberant symbolism was intended to suggest or even provoke ideas, he wanted his abstract designs to appear restful. 'Always leave your design in repose', Knox instructed Kingston students. 'Never leave anything with the feeling of movement, as a seed falling. Always keep your design quite flat.'[35]

His garden ornaments with their four handles or two feet and two handles and designed to stand on pedestals can be seen as crosses. Viewed from above, they are shaped like a nimbus within a cross. Knox naturally referred to Irish metalwork, manuscripts and the Manx crosses with their low-relief Borre ring-chain patterns. The *Sigurd* and *Beowulf* jardinières (illustrated on page 20, nos. 4 and 6) are shaped like a Borre brooch, or without their lug handles like a cauldron which to the Celts symbolised rebirth and resurrection – a more sinister tale that might have appealed more to Watts was that the Irish possessed a cauldron into which their dead soldiers were thrown, then cooked at night to rise and fight again the next day.[36] On the *Brunhild*, one of Knox's first terracotta designs, (illustrated opposite), restrained knotwork inspired by a pattern from the Braddan Cross at Kirk Braddan, is brought to a halt with a tiny Celtic coil transformed into an Art Nouveau tendril.[37]

Knox, *Brunhild* pot on *Gnomme* pedestal (© Christie's Images Ltd. 2005).

Knox, *Regin* pot and pedestals in Liberty & Co.'s *Book of Garden Ornaments*, 1904, identified by Watts as an anonymous Liberty design.

Except for a high-relief knot pattern or spiral that he would use as focal colour - like enamel on designs for Cymric silver – Knox's terracotta decoration was shallower than Compton pottery, raised only half an inch, incised and even pierced. Focal knots in the *Lindisfarne* and *Regin* jardinières appear to represent a pine cone inside which are seeds, similar in concept to the Watts Chapel doorway which symbolises renewal and immortality and the central 'I AM' motif on the chapel doorway shows that, on occasion Watts took inspiration from the flatter patterns of the seventh-century Dublin manuscript, the *Book of Durrow* to which he too referred. Knox wrote in 'Ancient Crosses in the Isle of Man' that a common Manx theme was a deer hunt, with dogs, horse and rider and huntsmen walking.[38] The *Gnomme* pedestal

Left: Watts, *Love and Death* panel from G. F. Watts's studio fireplace at Limnerslease, 1901.

Below: Watts, symbol of renewal, Watts Chapel doorway (detail), 1895-98.

decoration could be interpreted as dogs on the scent hunting through trees with birds in the upper branches, and the *Beowulf* as dogs and deer intertwined.[39] Perhaps because of the island's legendary links with superstition, the sense of mystery predominates over death. Watts's Highland heritage had revolved around violent battles; and at home with her delicate aging artist and in their work, death was an ever-present subject. But her terracotta version of G. F. Watts's peaceful interpretation of *Love and Death* is a pelican pierced through the heart by sword whose hilt bears the key of immortality.[40]

25

Knox, *Siegfried* pedestal and pot
in Liberty & Co.'s *Book of Garden Ornaments*, 1904.

Knox's terracotta patterns echo and extend Manx design which he described as two waved lines crossing and recrossing, without distinguishable motive, growing out of one wave, arranged symmetrically, encircling and attaching itself to the other. 'It expresses the very elementary sentiment of stability out of which the art of the builder grows.'[41] For Knox and Watts, the design at the base of their columns and pedestals was as significant as the upper, more prominent decoration, but to achieve balance and counter-balance, highlighting their patterns and exercising restraint, they left space undecorated. As well as paired motifs, notably the jewel-like medallions inside the chapel at Compton, Watts made use of *triskeles*, tripartite spirals that had magical connotations. These can be seen on a wellhead and adjoining a Borre-style gripping-beast pattern in the chapel's 'Golden Girdle of the Trinity'. [42]

Watts, Wellhead, Compton, 1906.

The interior decoration of the chapel, modelled in terracotta and gesso, with looser Art Nouveau whiplash, was painted in tempera and completed in April 1904 shortly before her husband's death. As her first apprentices were living in the hostel attached to the gallery she had had built to house his paintings, Watts named her Arts and Crafts community the Potters' Arts Guild. That year her terracotta was exhibited for Ireland at the World's Fair in St Louis, U.S.A., 'to show what can be done with Irish raw material' – the specially designed *St Louis* pot is yellower than the grey terracotta Watts introduced for houses built of stone.[43]

Potters' Arts Guild,
Season pot, c. 1905,
Duchess and *St Louis* pots, 1904,
Poppy bowl, 1908.

While the ornament on her tombstones, sundials and certain jardinières – the *Celtic* pot and stand, the *St Louis* and the sensuous swirling *Cobra* and *Eel* pots – was predominantly Celtic, those with heart motifs and the Guild's more Italianate pots, with foliate friezes and swags, were more restrained.[44] New designs produced by Carter's for Liberty & Co. catalogues had foliate decoration, although it is uncertain how

Potters Arts' Guild,
Floreat pot, c. 1902; Pedestal vase, c. 1901; *Cobra* pot, c. 1901;
Scroll pot, 1898; *Eel* pot, c. 1901; *Scroll* pot, 1898;
Celtic pot and stand, c. 1899.

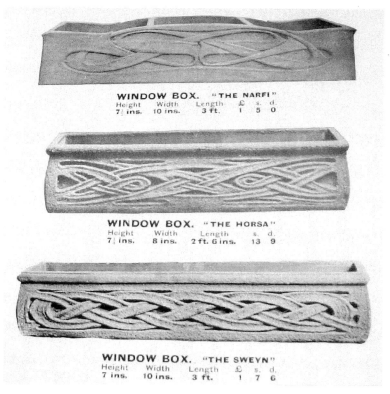

WINDOW BOX. "THE NARFI"

Height	Width	Length	£	s.	d.
7½ ins.	10 ins.	3 ft.	1	5	0

WINDOW BOX. "THE HORSA"

Height	Width	Length		s.	d.
7½ ins.	8 ins.	2 ft. 6 ins.		13	9

WINDOW BOX. "THE SWEYN"

Height	Width	Length	£	s.	d.
7 ins.	10 ins.	3 ft.	1	7	6

Liberty & Co., *Narfi, Horsa* and *Sweyn* window boxes,
Garden Pottery catalogue, 1905.

many of these were designed by Knox. The elongated interlace
he used in his metalwork was well suited to window boxes,
whether within their narrow confines or without, as in the
Narfi where it curves above the rectangular rim.[45]

The more expensive grey terracotta was introduced in
the 1905 catalogue. Liberty & Co. prices quoted in the 1904
Book of Garden Ornaments, (lowered in 1905 and restored to a
similar level in 1907) ranged from five shillings for Watts's
ten-inch *Scroll* to eleven guineas for a large Knox garden seat
and £20 13s. for his fountain and surround, or £23 15s. in
grey. His shrub box was marketed at five guineas in red and

Liberty & Co., 1905:
Above: *Merlin* fountain.
Below: *Tara* garden seat.

Knox, *Olaf* pot
and pedestal; *Thrym*
pot on *Gnomme* pedestal.
Watts, *Freïya* orange
tree box, 1904.

her octagonal *Freyia* orange tree box at ten. Their jardinières
were produced in various sizes and for an average one foot
four inches ranged from 15s. 6d. for Watts's *Lotus* – (sold in
two sizes, this size marketed by her guild as the *Artichoke* pot
sold for 10s.) – to £2 12s. 6d. for Knox's *Olaf*, which with its
pedestal cost six guineas and stood four feet high. Her sundials
ranged from £5 12s. 6d. to nine guineas. The best value Knox
pot and pedestal was the *Thrym* and *Gnomme* at £3 13s. 6d.,
overall height three feet seven inches, or the two-foot *Grimhild*
pot and stand combined at £1 10s.[46]

Liberty & Co., 'The New Garden Pottery',
terrace and jardinières designed by Knox and Watts, 1904-5.

The modern Celtic garden ornaments of Knox and Watts were marketed together by Liberty & Co. for only two years, until 1905 when their award-winning display, above, received a gold medal from the Royal Botanical Society and a Royal Horticultural Society silver medal.[47] The magnificent Knox balustrade served as a flower stand on Marylebone Station. Long after Liberty & Co. advertised his terracotta garden ware, this continued to be made at Carter & Co and inspired similar designs as late as 1921. Radley Young applied tin glazes to the two earliest pots, the *Thrym* and the *Brunhild*, which bears the stamp 'Carter & Co.'[48] The Potters' Arts Guild coloured ware – Art Nouveau saints, candlesticks, bedheads, bookends, plaques, vases, salad bowls and mugs painted in tempera in the vibrant colours of the chapel interior, waxed and stamped with a small circular 'PAG' mark – and produced at Compton at the same time as the garden ware, did not appear in Liberty & Co. catalogues.

Knox, Flower Stand at Marylebone Station
(Leicestershire Record Office).

34

Liberty & Co.,

Above: *Penda* pot, c. 1905
(Sotheby's).

Left: *Floralis* sundial, c. 1905
(Sotheby's).

Potters' Arts Guild,
Greek pot, c. 1912.

The guild introduced new designs, figures for gardens and memorials, and continued to exhibit widely, winning Royal Horticultural Society awards until 1912. Gertrude Jekyll was the only known outside designer to have a pot produced at Compton. Her *Jekyll Bowl* was illustrated in 1909; and on behalf of Sir Edwin Lutyens in 1921, she commissioned the guild to produce tiny versions of their jardinières for Queen Mary's dolls house. The Aldourie Potters' Arts Guild did not reopen after the First World War, by which time Watts had completed a second mortuary chapel scheme, for the Cambridge Military Chapel at Aldershot. [49]

Archibald Knox and Mary Seton Watts continued to develop imaginative Celtic memorials, which they infused with their own flamboyant Art Nouveau and later Art Deco influences. Potters' Arts Guild catalogues offered new garden pottery designs, but the early *Celtic* and *Scroll* pots remained in production at Compton until the pottery closed in 1955, long after Watts's death in 1938. Knox died in 1933. His teachings were perpetuated by the Knox Guild of Design and Craft (1913-39), founded by his former Kingston pupils, two sisters, Winifred Tuckfield and Denise Wren, who arranged annual exhibitions at the Kingston Art Gallery and in the 1920s at the Whitechapel Art Gallery in London.[50]

Knox had advised his Kingston students to 'aim at order: hope for beauty ... striving always for simpleness and breadth'. Watts aimed for beauty, hoped for order and in Compton war memorial achieved simplicity and breadth. There is no record that the two ever met, except in the union of their *Modern Celtic Art* garden pottery where now, as both intended, lichen grows in the crevices, generating a sense of 'perpetual sunset'.[51]

ACKNOWLEDGEMENTS

My grateful thanks to Stephen A. Martin, to Philip Bates, Nicola Gordon Bowe, Thelma Bowley of Poole Pottery, The Hon Mrs Judy Cameron and the late Colonel Angus Cameron, Yvonne Cresswell of Manx National Heritage, Audrey Draper, Lady Erskine, Jasmin French, Leslie Hayward, Richard Jefferies, Curator of the Watts Gallery, Kingston Museum and Heritage Centre, to Barbara Morris, Jennifer Opie, Jackie Rees, Emma Strouts, Baron Sweerts de Landas, Westminster City Archives, Rosemary Wren and Lorna Young.   VFG

Heart Pot.

Size	Height	Width	Price
A	1ft. 8in.	1ft. 9in.	£1 5 0
B	1ft. 6in.	1ft. 7in.	0 18 6
C	1ft. 4in.	1ft. 5in.	0 12 6
D	11½in.	1ft. 1in.	0 8 0
E	9¾in.	10½in.	0 5 0

Snake Pot.

Size	Height	Width	Price
A	1ft. 8in.	1ft. 9in.	£1 5 0
B	1ft. 6in.	1ft. 7in.	0 18 6
C	1ft. 4in.	1ft. 5in.	0 12 6
D	11½in.	1ft. 1in.	0 8 0
E	9¾in.	10½in.	0 5 0

Hanging Pot.

Height	Price
3ft. 4in.	£1 5 0

Oblong Italian Box.

Length	Width	Height	Price
16½in.	10½in.	7¾in.	£0 6 0

Poppy Box.

Size	Height	Width	Length	Price
A	8in.	9in.	20¼in.	£0 8 0
B	8in.	9in.	15in.	0 5 6

Square Italian Box.

Height	Square	Price
10in.	11in.	£0 8 0

Vine Pot.

Height	Width	Price
1ft. 4in.	1ft. 8in.	£0 12 6

The Artichoke Pot.

Size	Height	Width	Price
A	1ft. 7in.	2ft. 5in.	£1 4 0
B	1ft. 4in.	1ft. 8in.	0 10 0

Thong Pot.

Size	Height	Width	Price
A	1ft. 3½in.	12in.	£0 7 6
B	1ft. 1in.	10½in.	0 5 0

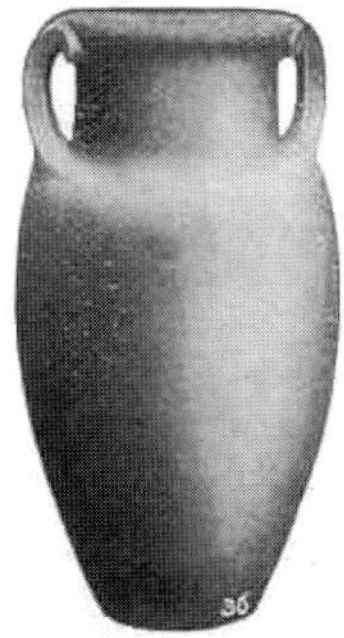

TWO SHAPES, VARIOUS SIZES AND PRICES.

Fold Pot.

Size	Height	Width	Price
C	12¾in.	1ft. 7½in.	£0 8 0
D	11 in.	1ft. 4½in.	0 6 0

Jekyll Bowl.

Size	Height	Width	Price
A	1ft. 4in.	2ft 2¼in.	15/–
B	1ft 2in.	1ft. 11¼in.	10/6
C	12¼in.	1ft. 8in.	8/–
D	10⅝in.	1ft. 5in.	5/–
E	8in.	1ft. ½in.	3/6

Flat Handle Pot.

Size	Height	Width	Price
A	10½in.	1ft. 1½in	5/–
B	9½in.	11½in.	3/6

Wall Pot.

Height	Width	Price
1ft. 5in.	2ft. 2½in.	£0 16 0

Celtic Bulb Bowl.

10in.	8in.	6in.	4½in.
4/6	3/6	3/-	2/-

St. Louis Pot.

Size	Height	Width	Price
A	16½in.	25½in.	£1 4 0
B	15in.	23in.	0 17 6
C	12½in.	19in.	0 10 0
D	9½in.	14½in.	0 6 0

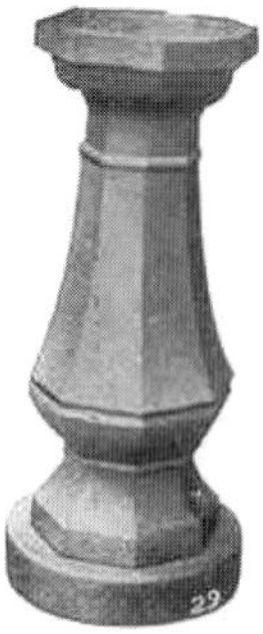

Octagonal Pedestal.

Height	Price
3ft.	£1 0 0

Bird Bath.

Handles & Scroll without Pedestal.

Size	Width	Height	Price
A	18in.	$3\frac{3}{4}$in.	£0 10 0
B	$15\frac{3}{4}$in.	$3\frac{3}{4}$in.	0 7 6
C	$13\frac{1}{2}$in.	3in.	0 6 0
D	$10\frac{1}{3}$in.	$2\frac{3}{4}$in.	0 4 0

Pedestals, various heights and designs, from 3/- to 21/-

Square Pedestal.

Height	Price
2ft. 6in.	£0 18 6

Tudor Sundial.

Height	Base
3ft. 7in.	1ft. 10in.

Price
£4 0 0

Shell Bird Bath.

Size	Width	Price
A	1ft. 6in.	£0 12 6
B	1ft. ...	0 4 6

Cobra Sundial.

Height	Base	Price
3ft. 8in.	2ft.	£4 0 0

With any Motto,

Tudor Pot.

Size	Height	Width	Price
A	2ft. ...	2ft. 6in.	£1 5 0
B	1ft. 5in.	1ft. 10in.	0 10 0

Bird Sundials.

Height	Base	Price
4ft. 6in.	3ft.	£6 10 0

Winged Hours Sundial.

Height	Base	Price
3ft. 4in.	2ft. square.	£5 0 0

and Heavy Brass Dial Plate.

Poppy Pot.

Size	Height	Width	Price
A	1ft. 10in.	2ft. 4in.	£1 5 0
B	1ft. 4in.	1ft. 8½in.	0 10 0

NOTES

[1] Liberty & Co., *Book of Garden Ornaments*, exh., cat., 1904, 3.

[2] Grafton Gallery, London, *Exhibition of Modern Celtic Art*, exh. cat., 1904.

[3] Watts Gallery, *Mary Seton Watts (1849-1938) Unsung Heroine of the Art Nouveau*, Veronica Franklin Gould, ed., exh. cat., 1998, 28, 48, 65 and 71.

[4] Mona Douglas, *This is Ellan Vannin*, 1996, 29.

[5] Archibald Knox, 'John Miller Nicholson', *Mannin*, vol. i, 1913, 25.

[6] 'The Isle of Man Natural History Proceedings' *The Arts and Industry in Victorian Isle of Man*, 1998, quoted in Martin Faragher *Knox, Nicholson and the Douglas Art School*, 2000 (typescript, Manx National Heritage).

[7] Christopher Frayling, *The Royal College of Art: 150 Years of Art & Design*, 1987, 55.

[8] P. M. C. Kermode, *Manx Crosses: A Catalogue of the Manx Crosses with Runic Inscriptions*, 1887.

[9] Archibald Knox, 'Ancient Crosses in the Isle of Man', *Builder*, lxv, 30 September 1893, 243.

[10] Knox, 'The Isle of Man as a Sketching Ground', *Studio*, vol. vii, 1896, 142-46.

[11] John Davey, ed. *M H Baillie Scott: The Surrey Contribution, Work of an Arts and Crafts Architect*, 1996, 10; Hermann Muthesius, *Das Englische Haus*, 1904, *The English House*, 1979, 51.

[12] Knox, *Antiquary*, 'Old Kirk Lonan, Isle of Man', vol. xxxiv, 1898, 15-19.

[13] Mary Seton Watts, *The Word in the Pattern*, 1898, 2000 edition, 2.

[14] J. Gleeson-White, 'A Mortuary Chapel, designed by Mrs G. F. Watts', *Studio*, vol. xiv, 1898, 235-40; Veronica Franklin Gould, *The Watts Chapel: An Arts & Crafts Memorial*, 1993, 2 and 22.

[15] Alexander Fraser Tytler, 'An Account of Some Extraordinary Structures on the Tops of Hills in the Highlands with Remarks on the Progress of the Arts among the Ancient Inhabitants', *Transactions of the Royal Society of Edinburgh*, II, 1790.

[16] Franklin Gould 1993, 16-17.

[17] Anna and Graham Ritchie, *Scotland: An Oxford Archaeological Guide*, 1998, 134 and 148.

[18] Watts Gallery, 1998, 18-20.

[19] Veronica Franklin Gould, *G. F. Watts: The Last Great Victorian*, 2004, 203.

[20] Ibid., 1993, 1, 4, 15, 39; Watts Gallery, 1998, 71.

[21] Mary Seton Watts, *Journal*, 1 October 1893 (Watts Gallery).

[22] Ibid, 14 November 1895.

[23] John Ruskin, 'The Lamp of Truth', *The Seven Lamps of Architecture*, 1949, xx.

[24] 'Notes from the Workshop,' Liberty & Co., 1904, 3-4.

[25] *Studio*, XVII, 1899, 103.

[26] Letter to Alexander Morton & Co's weavers at Killybegs, Donegal, 20 December 1899. (Archive of Art and Design); Watts, 2000, 15.

[27] Letter to James Morton, 15 March 1901 (Archive of Art and Design).

[28] Grafton Gallery, *Founding a National Industry: Irish Carpet Exhibition*, exh. cat, 1903.

[29] *Carter & Co Ltd., Poole* brochure, c. 1910; *Carter Products,*, 1921; Leslie Hayward and Paul Atterbury, *Poole Pottery: Carter & Company and their Successors 1873-1995*, 1995, 8-10.

[30] Liberty & Co., 1904, 4.

[31] 'The Potter's Wheel' *Country Life*, 15 March 1902, 328-30.

[32] Watts Gallery, 1998, 36-37.

[33] Quoted in Whitechapel Art Gallery, London, *Exhibition of the Knox Guild of Design and Craft*, exh. cat., 1923, 5-6.

[34] Winifred Tuckfield, *Mannin*, vol. vii, May 1916, 382.

[35] Kingston School of Art lecture, 23 September 1907.

[36] *Sacred Symbols: The Celts*, 1996; Liberty & Co., 1904, 10, 15 and 19.

[37] Knox, 1893, 243; Liberty & Co., 8 and 24.

[38] Knox, ibid..

[39] Liberty & Co., 1904, 8-10.

[40] Watts Gallery, 1998, 43.

[41] Knox, 1893, 243.

[42] Franklin Gould, 1993, 32; Watts Gallery, 1998, 57 and 66.

[43] *Irish Industrial Exhibition, World's Fair, St. Louis, II, Handbook and Catalogue to the Industrial Section*, 1904, exh. cat., 35.

[44] Watts Gallery, 1998, 51, 55 and 75.

[45] Liberty & Co., 1904, 35.

[46] Ibid; *Potters' Arts Guild, Price List of Pots and Sundials*, 1 May 1909.

[47] Ibid, 1905, 24.

[48] Barbara Morris, *Liberty Design 1874-1914*, 1989, 68-69; Martin, 2001, 276; Hayward and Atterbury, 1995, 22.

[49] *The Potters' Arts Guild Price List of Pots and Sundials*, 1 May 1909; Watts Gallery, 1898, 63 and 66.

[50] Rosemary D. Wren 'New Light from Old Records: Archibald Knox's Approach to his Work', Martin, 2001, 111-16.; Whitechapel Art Gallery, *Exhibition of the Knox Guild of Design and Craft*, exh. cats., 1921, 1923 and 1925.

[51] Knox, 1896, 146.

SELECT BIBLIOGRAPHY

Veronica Franklin Gould, *The Watts Chapel: An Arts & Crafts Memorial*, 1993.
– *G. F. Watts: The Last Great Victorian*, 2004.
J Gleeson-White, 'A Mortuary Chapel, designed by Mrs G. F. Watts,' *Studio*, vol XIV, 1898.
Grafton Gallery, London, *Exhibition of Modern Celtic Art*, exh. cat., 1904.
Leslie Hayward and Paul Atterbury, *Poole Pottery: Carter & Company and their Successors 1873-1995*, 1995.
Archibald Knox, 'Ancient Crosses in the Isle of Man', *Builder*, vol. lxv, 1893.
– 'Celtic Ornament', *Builder*, lxiv, 1893.
– 'Old Kirk Lonan, Isle of Man', *Antiquary*, vol. xxxiv, 1898.
Liberty & Co., *Book of Garden Ornaments*, exh. cat., 1904.
– *Garden Pottery*, exh. cats., 1905 and 1907.
Stephen A. Martin, ed, *Archibald Knox*, 2001.
Mary Seton Watts, *The Word in the Pattern*, 1898, 2000 edition.
Watts Gallery, *Mary Seton Watts (1849-1938) Unsung Heroine of the Art Nouveau*, Veronica Franklin Gould, ed., exh. cat., 1998.

PICTURE CREDITS

Christie's Images Ltd. 23; Leicestershire Record Office 34; Manx National Heritage 5 (left); Leslie Hayward 20 (above); City of Westminster Archives Centre 20 (below), 30, 31, 33; private collections 15, 25, 27; Sotheby's 35; Watts Gallery 5 (right); William Morris Gallery 38–41.

INDEX